Elephant Calves

Julie Murray

Abdo
BABY ANIMALS
Kids

abdopublishing.com

Published by Abdo Kids, a division of ABDO, PO Box 398166, Minneapolis, Minnesota 55439.
Copyright © 2018 by Abdo Consulting Group, Inc. International copyrights reserved in all countries.
No part of this book may be reproduced in any form without written permission from the publisher.

Printed in the United States of America, North Mankato, Minnesota.

052017

092017

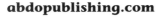

THIS BOOK CONTAINS
RECYCLED MATERIALS

Photo Credits: iStock, Shutterstock

Production Contributors: Teddy Borth, Jennie Forsberg, Grace Hansen

Design Contributors: Christina Doffing, Candice Keimig, Dorothy Toth

Publisher's Cataloging in Publication Data

Names: Murray, Julie, 1969-, author.

Title: Elephant calves / by Julie Murray.

Description: Minneapolis, Minnesota : Abdo Kids, 2018 | Series: Baby animals |
    Includes bibliographical references and index.

Identifiers: LCCN 2016962292 | ISBN 9781532100024 (lib. bdg.) |
    ISBN 9781532100710 (ebook) | ISBN 9781532101267 (Read-to-me ebook)

Subjects: LCSH: Elephants--Juvenile literature. | Elephants--Infancy--Juvenile literature.

Classification: DDC 599.67--dc23

LC record available at http://lccn.loc.gov/2016962292

Table of Contents

Elephant Calves

A baby elephant is a calf.

The calf is big! It is three feet (91.4 cm) tall. It weighs about 200 pounds (90.7 kg).

It stays close to its mom.

The **herd** helps protect it.

It drinks its mother's milk.

Soon it will eat plants too.

It has a long trunk. It holds its mother's tail.

The trunk is like an arm.

The calf touches its mom.

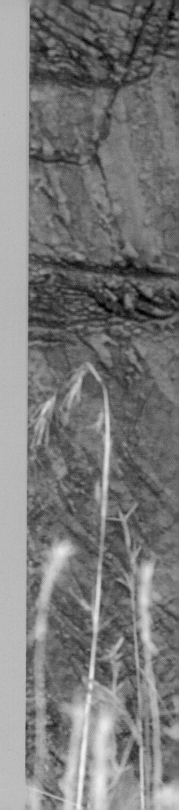

It has **wrinkly** skin. This keeps the calf cool.

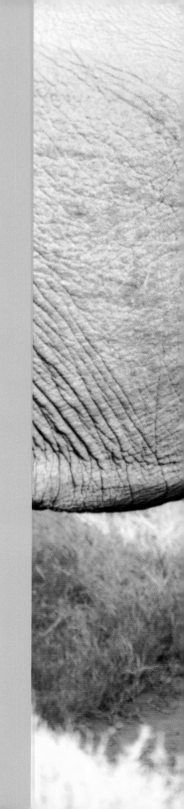

The calf has two big ears.

It uses them like a fan.

The calf grows slowly.

It can live for 70 years!

Watch an Elephant Calf Grow!

newborn

5–10 years

11–17 years

18 years

Glossary

herd
a large group of animals that live, feed, and move together.

wrinkly
having many lines or folds.

Index

abdokids.com

Use this code to log on to abdokids.com and access crafts, games, videos, and more!

Abdo Kids Code:
BEK0024